THE CREATIVE COOK

Splendid

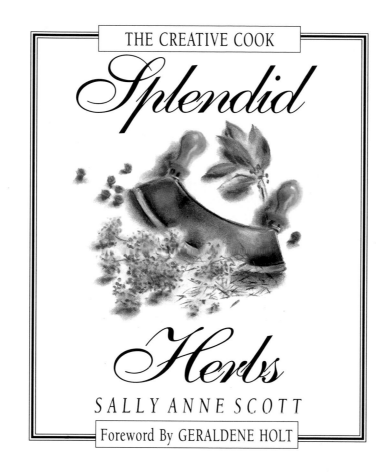

Herbs

SALLY ANNE SCOTT

Foreword By GERALDENE HOLT

COLE
GROUP

To David with thanks for his inspiration in and
out of the kitchen.

Please note the following:

Quantities given in all the recipes serve 4 people unless otherwise stated.

Butter and margarine are packaged in a variety of forms, including 1-pound blocks and ¼-pound sticks. A stick equals 8 tablespoons (½ cup).

Cream used is specified as light cream (containing from 18 percent to 30 percent milk fat), whipping cream (30 percent to 36 percent milk fat), or heavy cream (at least 36 percent milk fat).

Flour used is all-purpose flour, unless otherwise specified.

Preparation of ingredients, such as the cleaning, trimming, and peeling of vegetables and fruit, is presumed and the text refers to any aspect of this only if unusual, such as onions used unpeeled, etc.

Citrus fruit should be thoroughly washed to remove any agricultural residues. For this reason, whenever a recipe uses the rind of any citrus such as oranges, lemon, or limes, the text specifies washed fruit. Wash the fruit thoroughly, rinse well, and pat dry. If using organically grown fruit, rinse briefly and pat dry.

Eggs used are large unless otherwise specified. Because of the risk of contamination with salmonella bacteria, current recommendations from health professionals are that children, pregnant women, people on immuno-suppressant drugs, and the elderly should not eat raw or lightly cooked eggs. This book includes recipes with raw and lightly cooked eggs. These recipes are marked by an ★ in the text.

Editorial Direction: Lewis Esson Publishing
Art Director: Mary Evans
Design: Sue Storey
Illustrations: Alison Barratt
Food for Photography: Meg Jansz
Styling: Jane Newdick
Editorial Assistant: Penny David
American Editor: Norma MacMillan
Production: Jill Macey

Text copyright © Sally Anne Scott 1993
Foreword copyright © Geraldene Holt 1993
Photography copyright © Pia Tryde 1993
Design and layout copyright © Conran Octopus 1993

Published by Cole Group
4415 Sonoma Highway/PO Box 4089
Santa Rosa, CA 95402–4089
(707) 538–0492   FAX (707) 538–0497

First published in 1992 by
Conran Octopus Limited,
37 Shelton Street, London   WC2H 9HN

A   B   C   D   E   F   G   H
3   4   5   6   7   8   9   0

ISBN 1–56426–653–2
Library of Congress Cataloguing in process

Typeset by Servis Filmsetting Ltd
Printed and bound in Hong Kong

Distributed to the book trade by Publishers Group West

CONTENTS

FOREWORD

For me, few cooking ingredients give such profound pleasure as fresh herbs. The intense aroma of chopped mint leaves added to a lemon sauce or of bright green sweet basil torn into shreds for a tomato salad is both alluring and appetizing. I also never fail to be surprised by the transformation in the flavor of a dish by the addition of just a sprig of, say, tarragon or rosemary. The right herb not only complements the flavor of other ingredients in cooking but reveals their true flavor.

Herbs have long been part of our culinary history. Some are native wild plants. Others have been introduced. Today, no self-respecting cook's garden is cultivated without, at least, a clump of parsley and a patch of mint.

Yet we often remain wary of utilizing to the full these important plants. Cooks are sometimes concerned that the flavor of an herb will overwhelm or spoil a dish. If you are hesitant about cooking with herbs, add just a small amount – such as a lovage or bay leaf – to a homemade soup or stew. Then gradually experiment with other kinds: Stir chopped dill into a sauce for salmon or some coriander (cilantro) leaves into a dish of cooked potatoes. Add small sprigs of herbs like arugula, chervil, and ginger mint to a salad. Finally, progress to those characterful sauces like Genoese *pesto* and pungent Montpellier butter that depend on a sizable handful of herbs for their identity and richness.

So familiar are some of the accustomed herbal associations that cooks can be reluctant to develop new ideas. Take, for instance, the handsome felty-leaved sage; now sage is such an excellent herb in its well-known role (combined with onion and bread crumbs) in a stuffing for poultry, that we easily forget that chopped fresh sage is also a fine herb for adding to cheese dishes or to a sauce for pasta, or for flavoring breads.

Although it is quite common to add herbs to savory dishes, it is worth remembering that in European cooking of the time of Queen Elizabeth I, sweet dishes, too, were flavored with aromatic herbs. I think of the heavenly fragrance of the rose-scented geranium or mauve lavender blossoms, or the bewitching flavors of lemon verbena, elderberry flower, and pineapple sage, and how well they perfume cream, custards, and sorbets.

Once you have gained confidence in cooking with herbs, you will find that ideas dawn for your own delicious dishes. Your cooking will become more adventurous and lively because fresh herbs give dishes a uniquely satisfying and individual character that will be appreciated by both yourself and those for whom you cook.

GERALDENE HOLT

INTRODUCTION

*H*erbs have played an essential part in our lives for centuries. From their earliest instinctive use in primitive tribal magic, they came eventually to be systematically studied and dispensed by apothecaries and physicians, and grown in monastery gardens. John Gerard, in his great *Herball* of 1597, described the supposed properties of over 1,100 types. Now in modern-day herbalism, homeopathy, and aromatherapy, herbs have found renewed respect in all forms.

The culinary use of herbs has also been fairly continuous, although until recently we had become somewhat unadventurous, sticking only to a well-tried handful such as parsley, sage, and thyme. Now, however, we are thankfully rediscovering the exciting and delicious flavors of these wonderfully versatile plants and using them to enhance our food on a daily basis.

The proven medicinal qualities of herbs can also benefit us in many ways when incorporated regularly in our diets. Stronger flavored herbs can be used as an alternative to ordinary seasonings and can thus help to cut down our salt intake. They can also help offset the possible blandness of low-fat and high-fiber dishes.

BUYING, GROWING, AND PRESERVING HERBS

Most herbs sold commercially are preserved by drying. As a general rule, dried herbs are more potent than fresh. A good rule of thumb is to use three times as much fresh as dried.

It is now increasingly easy to buy fresh herbs all year round – either cut in bunches or growing in tiny pots. It is, however, also very simple and fun to grow – and dry – your own. Space is not always vital, since many are very happy in window boxes, on balconies, in a tiny garden, or even on the roof. Picking should always be on a sunny dry day, when the flowers are just about to appear, as this ensures the fullest flavors and retains most of the aromatic essential oils. Try not to bruise the leaves too much.

Drying can be done by tying the herbs in small bunches, then hanging them in a dust-free, light, and airy space – warm, but out of direct sunlight. Herbs with seed heads, such as dill, or coriander, should have small bags tied over them into which the seeds can be shaken. They will fall naturally, or can be gently rubbed to hasten the process.

Most herbs can also be frozen, although not all are suitable and I feel that there is at least a 20 percent loss of flavor in most cases. Place the fresh herbs in cellophane bags or small plastic tubs. Small amounts can be chopped and frozen in ice-cube trays for easily separable small quantities. Basil, marjoram, chives, and parsley are the best survivors of this method of preservation, but remember that they will always lose their color.

STORING AND PREPARING HERBS

Dried herbs should be kept in cool places well away from sunlight in order to preserve their essential oils – little glass jars in spice racks above the stove is exactly how *not* to store them! Buy them from stores with a rapid turnover and mark the date of purchase on the container, as their flavoring properties do not last much more than about 6 months.

Fresh herbs can either be kept in plastic bags in the refrigerator crisper, or if they have intact stems, stand them like flowers in a vase or glass of water.

Preparation of herbs is usually fairly straightforward. Fresh leaves are normally minced or snipped with scissors directly into a dish. Some, like basil, cooks prefer to tear rather than cut as this is held to preserve more of the oils. If you are in the habit of cutting large amounts of herbs, it is worth investing in a mezzaluna – a double-handled crescent-shaped knife – with a bowl curved to match the blade. Alternatively, a careful hand on the pulse of a food processor can cut down time and effort.

Seeds are usually lightly crushed in a mortar with a pestle before use or crushed to a powder in a spice or coffee mill or in a food processor.

CHOOSING THE RIGHT HERB

After exhausting all the tried-and-tested classic combinations – like sage and onion, peas and mint, lamb and rosemary, etc. – many people are quite bewildered by the sheer diversity of choice and are reluctant to experiment with herbs for fear of making expensive mistakes. I hope the recipes in this book will provide some ideas of ways to go. Also note the herb use in favorite foreign food – lemongrass in Thai food, basil in pasta and pizza sauces, etc. – and take a lead from them. Don't forget to look at old recipe books for ideas – even Mrs. Beeton included lemon thyme, marjoram, winter savory, and basil in her basic "herb powder for flavouring."

Angelica *(Angelica archangelica)*
Stems are candied for cake decoration and for flavoring custards and some soft white cheeses.

Anise *(Pimpinella anisum)*
Pungent in flavor. Crushed seeds used in cakes, cookies, fruit desserts, soups, and fish dishes. Very good digestive properties. Leaves used with fruit.

Arugula *(Eruca sativa)*
This member of the mustard family, very popular in Elizabethan cooking, is now enjoying a well-deserved revival in popularity as a salad addition.

Basil *(Ocimum basilicum)*
Extremely versatile with a warm Latin American, spicy flavor. Leaves are used to best effect with tomatoes, either shredded raw over salads or cooked in pasta sauces. The flavor also works well in dishes with garlic and wine and in creamy sauces. Several varieties with subtly different flavors, one lemon-scented.

Bay *(Laurus nobilis)*
One of the most used culinary herbs and an essential ingredient for bouquet garni. Fresh or dried leaves work particularly well in stocks, casseroles, pâtés, game and poultry dishes, and in pickling.

Bergamot *(Monarda didyma)*
Highly perfumed leaves good in small quantities for stuffings, salads, and sweet dishes and for making a herbal tea.

Borage *(Borago officinalis)*
Flowers candied for cake decoration, while leaves used in salads and stuffings and for fritters. Popular for refreshing summer fruit drinks.

Caraway *(Carum carvi)*
Aromatic seeds crushed for flavoring cakes, cookies, breads, cheese, cabbage, stews, and salads.

Celery *(Apium graveolens)*
Leaves used in salads and soups and in poultry stuffings and fish sauces. Seeds used in pickling and to flavor stews and curried dishes. Ground and sold as celery salt, useful for low-sodium diets.

Chervil *(Anthriscus cerefolium)*
Delicately flavored leaves are an ingredient of fines herbes. Flavor goes well in salads and dressings, with vegetables, fish, and eggs.

Chives *(Allium schoenoprasum)*
Flower heads used for garnish. Delicate onion-flavored leaves best used raw or lightly cooked especially as a garnish for soups, salads, and egg dishes. Also for meat, fish, poultry, and vegetable dishes and in cheese mixtures, dips, and dressings.

Cilantro/Coriander *(Coriandrum sativum)*
Distinctive earthy flavor of fresh leaves used in Indian, Latin American, Thai, and other Asian cuisines. Now popular in salads and sauces. Crushed seeds (coriander) much used in Mediterranean dishes, such as ratatouille, terrines and pâtés.

Cumin *(Cuminum cyminum)*
Perfumed seeds, whole or ground, widely used in Middle-Eastern, Indian, and Latin American dishes based on beef, lamb, chicken, and eggplant. Common in pickles and chutneys.

Dill *(Anethum graveolens)*
Delicate flavor of fresh leaves works well with potatoes and cucumber and in salads and dressings. Also marries particularly well with fish and seafood and widely used in sauces and marinades.

Elder *(Sambucus nigra)*
Flowers impart their delicious flavor, akin to that of the muscat grape, to a wide variety of sweet dishes and preserves.

Fennel *(Foeniculum vulgare)*
Delicate anise flavor of leaves is popular with fish, especially as a stuffing for oily fish. Crushed seeds used similarly. Also aids digestion of fat; is often used with fatty meat like pork.

Garlic *(Allium sativum)*
Related to the onion, this bulb is one of the world's most widely used flavorings. Popular minced raw in sauces and dressings, it also features in a wide variety of cooked dishes.

Geranium, scented (*Pelargonium*)
Leaves of different types have distinct delicate flavors: There are varieties with a rose scent, others with the flavors of oranges and apples. Used to flavor gelatin desserts, cakes, and custards, as well as summer drinks.

Horseradish (*Cochlearia armoracia*)
Hot and pungent taste of this root is traditional with roast beef. It also marries well with salmon, trout, and mackerel and is good in fish pâtés. An aid to digestion, it is popular with fatty meats and fish.

Hyssop (*Hyssopus officinalis*)
Bitter leaves used sparingly in salads and in soups, stews, and casseroles. Flowers are used in salads.

Juniper (*Juniperus communis*)
Berries from this conifer are mild and resinous. Culinary application is limited, but they work well with game and in pâtés and are used in pickling.

Lavender (*Lavandula spica*)
Strongly scented flowers are candied for cake decoration or used to flavor jams and jellies.

Lemon balm (*Melissa officinalis*)
Delicate lemony leaves used in soups, salads, fish and poultry dishes, in custards, gelatin desserts and fruit compotes. Also in fruit and wine drinks.

Lemongrass (*Cymbopogon citratus*)
This Southeast Asian perennial has a strong lemon flavor and is popular in the cooking of the region. Dried and crushed it is known as *sereh* and has long been available in Asian grocers. The fresh stalks are also now found in many supermarkets.

Lemon verbena (*Aloysia triphylla*)
Highly perfumed leaves used sparingly to give lemon tang to poultry and fish dishes, milk puddings, fruit salads, sweet sauces, and jams.

Lovage (*Levisticum officinale*)
Spicy celery flavor of leaves good with legumes and in soups, casseroles, cheese dishes, and sauces. Earthy taste of seeds also used to flavor potato and rice dishes as well as breads and pastries.

Marigold (*Calendula officinalis*)
Fresh flower petals used for salads and as garnish. Dried they are used like saffron to give flavor and color to cheese, rice, and fish dishes, to soups and stews, cakes, and custards.

Marjoram and oregano (*Origanum*)
Delicate sweet-scented leaves of sweet marjoram (*O. majorana*) used fresh in salads and raw vegetable dishes and added to fish and meat dishes at the end of cooking. More robust French or pot marjoram (*O. onites*) and oregano (*O. vulgare*) dry well and are popular in the cooking of the Mediterranean countries, especially on Italian pizzas and in pasta sauces and Greek salads.

Mint (*Mentha*)
Family of refreshing leaves with delightfully different flavors. As well as familiar spearmint and peppermint, there are varieties that taste of apple, lemon, basil, eau de cologne, pineapple, and ginger. Used widely in ice-creams and fruit dishes; also in savory dishes, especially with lamb, green peas, and potatoes.

Nasturtium (*Tropaeolum majus*)
Leaves used to add distinctive peppery flavor to salads, sauces, and sandwiches, while flowers can be a colorful and unusual garnish. Seeds and buds used in pickles.

Parsley (*Petroselinum crispum*)
Probably most widely used culinary herb and base of bouquet garni. Best used raw or briefly cooked in soups, salads, sauces, and fish and egg dishes. Flat-leaf variety, also called Italian parsley, has a stronger flavor than the curly-leaf.

Primrose (*Primula vulgaris*)
Fresh primrose flowers and young leaves can be used in salads and to flavor wine and preserves, as well as some puddings and sorbets.

Purslane (*Portulaca oleracea*)
Young leaves can be used in salads and to flavor cheese and egg dishes and dips.

Rosemary *(Rosmarinus officinalis)*
Pungently flavored resinous leaves used sparingly in stews, roasts, and marinades, especially in conjunction with lamb, pork, and game. They can also be infused in milk for custards and used to flavor fruit desserts. Flowers are added fresh to salads or candied for a garnish.

Sage *(Salvia officinalis)*
Strongly aromatic leaves are used with pork, veal, game, liver, and fatty meats. Also good with fresh beans, legumes, and cheeses. The many varieties have varying degrees of pungency, one even tasting of pineapple. The flowers are used in salads.

Salad burnet *(Poterium sanguisorba)*
Delicate flavor of leaf imparts nutty, cooling cucumber flavor to salads and raw vegetable dishes. Also works well with soft cheeses, in creamy soups, egg dishes, and in savory mousses.

Savory, winter and summer *(Satureja montana and S. hortensis)*
Used like sage, summer savory leaves are traditionally teamed with fresh and dried beans, or used to flavor sausages, meat pies, and soups. Winter savory is combined with other herbs in sauces for game, duck, and pork.

Sorrel *(Rumex scutatus/acetosa)*
Similar to spinach, leaves used sparingly in salads. Also good in egg dishes and sauces for fish and with potatoes, onions, tomatoes, lamb, and beef.

Sweet cicely/myrrh *(Myrrhis odorata)*
Delicate sweet flavor of leaves and unripe seeds (fruit) have a hint of aniseed and are good in fruit tarts, salads, ice-creams, and sorbets. Particularly good with tart fruit such as rhubarb and gooseberry. Leaves are also used in salads and omelettes.

Sweet violet *(Viola odorata)*
Delicately flavored flowers added fresh to salads, used in fruit and wine cups, or infused to make syrup to flavor cakes, custards, and ice-creams. Flowers also candied for cake decorations.

Tarragon *(Artemisia dracunculus)*
One of the fines herbes, French tarragon has a wonderfully warm, subtle flavor that goes particularly well with chicken, eggs, and potatoes. It is also popular in salad dressings and sauces. Russian tarragon has coarser flavor.

Thyme *(Thymus)*
Essential ingredient in bouquet garni; has a strong flavor that develops on long, slow cooking, especially with garlic, olive oil, tomatoes, onion, and wine. Many different varieties with flavors to suit different uses; several are lemon-scented and work well with fish, seafood, and chicken.

HERB COMBINATIONS
Bouquet garni
Basic constituents are a bunch of parsley stems, 2 or 3 sprigs of thyme, and 1 or 2 bay leaves. They are commonly tied together with string or in a cheesecloth sack so that they can easily be removed after cooking. Dried versions are available.

Bouquets garnis are used in almost all stocks, sauces, soups, and stews. Apart from these basic constituents, there may also be additional ingredients, such as marjoram, fennel, tarragon, celery, savory, sage, garlic, leek, juniper, and lemon and orange zest, according to the dish in which the bouquet garni is being used. Rosemary is always included in Provençal bouquets.

Fine herbes
Chopped fresh parsley, tarragon, chives, and chervil, usually in equal quantities, form the most usual ingredients of this classic French flavoring. It is used in omelettes and other egg dishes, with soft cheese and cooked vegetables and in herb butters.

Herbes de Provence
This combination traditionally consists of bay, thyme, rosemary, basil, and savory. Most usually encountered dried, the mixture is particularly favored for use with grilled meats and poultry.

SOUPS

Soups make a wonderful showplace for herbs. Whether in as simple a form as sprinkling chopped chives, parsley, or cilantro on a cream soup just before serving or by incorporating at an early stage of cooking the flavor of a strongly aromatic herb like lemongrass or horseradish, the addition of herbs can transform a soup entirely. Dried herbs used at the outset enliven an insipid stock or bland ingredients. Fresh herbs given the briefest of cooking or stirred in at the last minute bring sparkle to any soup. One or two handfuls of chopped mixed fresh herbs in a good stock make one of the tastiest and most refreshing of soups, without the need for any other additional ingredients save some sour cream to give body. Serve this hot or chilled.

Left: Chilled Avocado Soup with Cilantro (page 14); center: Chilled Celery Root and Apple Soup with Chives (page 14)

CHILLED AVOCADO SOUP WITH CILANTRO

SERVES 4

*2 ripe avocados
juice of ½ lemon
1 tsp chili oil
3 tbsp minced fresh cilantro
1 cup thick plain yogurt
1¼ cups crème fraîche or sour cream
1¼ cups fresh tomato juice
2 cups vegetable stock
½ onion, finely shredded
salt and freshly ground black pepper*

Halve and pit the avocados. Peel them and place the flesh in a large bowl with the lemon juice. Mash until smooth. Stir in the chili oil and two-thirds of the cilantro. Cover and chill 30 minutes.

Gently blend in the yogurt and crème fraîche, followed by the tomato juice and finally the stock. Stir in the shredded onion and season. Chill 2 hours.

Adjust the seasoning, if necessary, and garnish with the remaining cilantro before serving.

CHILLED CELERY ROOT AND APPLE SOUP WITH CHIVES

SERVES 4

*4 tbsp butter
1½ large onions, sliced
½ tsp freshly grated nutmeg
3 firm, tart, green-skinned apples, unpeeled and
coarsely chopped
1 celery root, peeled and cut into small cubes
3 chicken bouillon cubes
2 tsp lime juice
salt and freshly ground black pepper
bunch of fresh chives*

Melt the butter in a large heavy saucepan over medium heat and sauté the onions until translucent, 2–4 minutes.

Sprinkle in the nutmeg and cook 1 minute longer. Add the apples and celery root and cook 5 minutes more, stirring constantly.

Dissolve the chicken bouillon cubes in 5 cups of hot water and add this to the pan. Reduce the heat, cover, and simmer 30 minutes.

Remove the pan from the heat and let cool a little before adding the lime juice. When cold, purée the soup in a blender or food processor. Then chill overnight.

Adjust the seasoning of the chilled soup and pour it into serving bowls. Finely snip the chives over the bowls to garnish.

HERBED CREAM OF CARROT SOUP

SERVES 4–6

1 lb carrots, chopped
2 cups vegetable stock
2 tbsp butter
1 large onion, diced
1 tsp celery salt
1¼ cups light cream
freshly ground black pepper
½ tbsp each minced watercress, parsley, and chives

Put the carrots and vegetable stock in a large saucepan and slowly bring to a boil. Reduce the heat, cover, and simmer until the carrots are tender, about 15 minutes. Remove from the heat and let cool.

Melt the butter in a frying pan over medium heat and sauté the onion until translucent. Add the celery salt and stir thoroughly. Remove from the heat and let cool.

Transfer the carrots and their stock to a blender or food processor. Add the onion and blend until smooth.

Return this to the saucepan and bring almost to a boil. Remove from the heat and add the cream. Season with pepper only and stir over low heat just to warm through. Do not allow to boil or the cream will curdle.

Pour the soup into warmed bowls and sprinkle a little of each of the 3 herbs over each serving.

HERBED VEGETABLE SOUP WITH VERMICELLI

SERVES 6

1 tbsp butter
1 large onion, diced
2 crisp celery stalks, chopped
2 large carrots, chopped
2 heads of broccoli, chopped
1 large potato, diced
1 tbsp chopped fresh oregano
1½ quarts vegetable stock
3 oz vermicelli
salt and freshly ground black pepper
1 tbsp chopped fresh flat-leaf parsley
1 tbsp chopped fresh chives

Melt the butter in a large heavy saucepan over medium heat and sauté the onion until translucent.

Add the other vegetables and sauté 5 minutes, stirring constantly. Add the oregano and sauté 2 minutes longer.

Add the stock and bring it slowly to a boil. Cover and simmer 10 minutes over low heat.

Add the vermicelli, increase the heat to medium again, and cook until the vermicelli is tender.

Adjust the seasoning. Add the parsley and chives just before serving.

LEMONGRASS is native to Southeast Asia, and its citrus tang is a basic flavor in much of the cooking of the area, especially Thai cuisine. It remains fibrous even after lengthy cooking so it is best removed after it has imparted its flavor. Once available only from speciality markets, or in its powdered form, known as SEREH, the long pale green stalks with bulbous bases are now a common sight in many supermarkets

FINNAN HADDIE is smoked haddock. Originally a British specialty, it is also produced in New England.

ARTICHOKE SOUP WITH LEMONGRASS

SERVES 6

2 stalks of lemongrass
1 lb large Jerusalem artichokes (sunchokes), unpeeled and coarsely chopped
6 tbsp butter
2 large onions, sliced
1 garlic clove, minced
5 cups chicken stock
¼ cup light cream (optional)
salt and freshly ground black pepper
1 tbsp minced fresh parsley, for garnish

Bring a large pan of water to a boil.

Crush the bulb ends of the lemongrass stalks, then place them in the pan of water with the artichokes and simmer 10 minutes. Drain the artichokes, reserving the lemongrass.

Melt the butter in a large heavy saucepan over medium heat. Add the onions and garlic and sauté about 3 minutes. Reduce the heat, cover, and simmer 5 minutes.

Add the pieces of artichoke and stir them into the onions and garlic. Then add the stock and bring to a boil. Add the reserved lemongrass, cover, and simmer 20 minutes. Remove from heat and let cool. Remove and discard the lemongrass.

Purée the mixture in a blender or food processor. Return it to the pan and reheat gently. Stir in the cream, if using, and adjust the seasoning.

Pour the soup into warmed serving bowls and garnish with parsley.

FISH CHOWDER WITH HORSERADISH

SERVES 6

1 lb skinned cod fillet
1 lb skinned finnan haddie fillet
5 cups milk
1 lb potatoes, peeled and diced
2½ cups fish stock
4 tbsp butter
½ lb onions, sliced
1 tbsp finely grated fresh horseradish
juice of ½ lemon
salt and freshly ground black pepper
½ cup drained canned whole-kernel corn (optional)

Put the fish in a large saucepan and cover with the milk. Bring to just below a boil over medium heat and simmer gently 20 minutes, or until the flesh flakes readily.

In another pan, combine the potatoes and fish stock. Bring to a boil and simmer 15 minutes.

Melt the butter in a frying pan over medium heat and sauté the onions until translucent, about 5 minutes.

Pour the potatoes and their stock into the fish pan, then add the onions in their butter. Sprinkle the horseradish on top and mix gently. Add the lemon juice.

Slowly bring the contents of the pan to a simmer and cook very gently for 15 minutes over very low heat. Season and add the corn, if using.

Pour into warmed bowls and serve immediately.

Clockwise from the left: Herbed Cream of Carrot Soup (page 15), Artichoke Soup with Lemongrass, and Fish Chowder with Horseradish

As well as being a refreshing and unusual appetizer, the CHILLED RASPBERRY AND MINT SOUP *makes an excellent palate cleanser between courses.*

The very fine green LENTILS FROM LE PUY *in France are actually almost purple in color. They have an incomparable flavor and cook very quickly. If none are available use any green lentils, but they will need longer cooking.*

GREEN LENTIL SOUP WITH HERBES DE PROVENCE

SERVES 4

1 ¼ cups green lentils, preferably Le Puy
2 tbsp butter
1 large onion, coarsely chopped
½ lb tomatoes, coarsely chopped
1 tbsp herbes de Provence
salt and freshly ground black pepper
1 tbsp chopped fresh flat-leaf parsley, for garnish

Wash the lentils thoroughly, then put them in a large heavy saucepan with 3½ cups of water. Bring

Chilled Raspberry and Mint Soup.

to a boil, then simmer gently until the lentils are tender, 15–20 minutes. Set them aside in their stock.

Melt the butter in a frying pan over medium heat and add the onion. Sauté until translucent, then add the tomatoes and herbs and stir constantly for 5 minutes. Transfer the contents of the frying pan to the lentil pan. Season, cover, and let cool.

When cool, purée the soup in a blender or food processor or push it through a strainer. Return to a medium heat and gently warm it through. Serve in warmed bowls, sprinkled with parsley.

CHILLED RASPBERRY AND MINT SOUP★

SERVES 4

juice of ½ lemon
3 pints raspberries
1 tbsp light brown sugar
1 egg yolk
(★see page 2 for advice on eggs)
½ cup plain yogurt
1 tbsp finely chopped fresh lemon mint
salt and freshly ground black pepper
4 mint sprigs, for garnish

Place all the ingredients in a blender or food processor, together with 1¼ cups of water. Blend 2 minutes. Strain the purée.

Chill at least 2 hours. Season lightly and serve garnished with the whole mint sprigs.

CLEAR SEAFOOD SOUP WITH SALICORNIA

SERVES 4

1 tsp sugar
4 dried shiitake mushrooms
3½ cups beef or chicken consommé
¼ lb fresh salicornia
3 oz each freshly cooked shucked hardshell clams and mussels and peeled small shrimp
freshly ground black pepper
2 tbsp minced young leeks, for garnish
2 tbsp minced fresh chives, for garnish

Dissolve the sugar in a little warm water. Add the mushrooms and soak 30 minutes.

Remove the mushrooms from the water and squeeze gently to remove excess liquid. Cut away any tough stems and then slice the caps thinly.

Put the consommé in a large saucepan and add the sliced mushrooms and the salicornia. Bring to a boil and simmer for 5 minutes.

Add the seafood, cover, and simmer 5 minutes longer. Season with pepper (salt should not be necessary due to the high mineral content of the salicornia).

Ladle the soup into 4 warmed bowls, sprinkle with leeks and chives, and serve immediately.

CHICKEN, LEMON, AND RICE SOUP WITH BAY★

SERVES 6–8

2 tbsp butter
¼ cup flour
thinly pared zest and juice of 3 large washed lemons
4 bay leaves
2 egg yolks
(★see page 2 for advice on eggs)
1¼ cups coarsely chopped cooked chicken meat
¾ cup cooked brown rice
salt and freshly ground black pepper

Melt the butter in a large heavy saucepan over medium heat. Stir in the flour and cook 3 minutes, stirring constantly. Slow add 7½ cups of water, whisking constantly to avoid lumps. Add the lemon zest and bay leaves and simmer gently 20 minutes.

In a large bowl, beat the egg yolks and slowly add the lemon juice, stirring constantly.

Remove the pan from the heat and slowly strain the liquid into the eggs, whisking gently. Return the mixture to the pan and bring to a very gentle simmer. Be careful not to let the soup boil at any stage or the egg will curdle.

Add the chicken and rice and season lightly. Let warm through 1–2 minutes and then serve in warmed bowls.

SHIITAKE MUSHROOMS *have been cultivated by the Japanese on oak bark for centuries. Both fresh and dried shiitake are available in many supermarkets.*

SALICORNIA, *also called marsh samphire, is a crisp sea plant found along the Pacific and Atlantic coasts.*

APPETIZERS AND SNACKS

Appetizers should excite the palate to prepare it for what is to come. What better way to ensure this than to tease it with the intriguing complexity of the flavors of herbs? First courses also make fairly safe testing grounds to try more unusual flavor combinations. Moreover, some herbs are known to have properties that excite the digestive processes and encourage the assimilation of food: For instance, the rosemary in *Gruyère, Rosemary, and Tomato Toasties* helps the digestion of the cooked cheese. For those cooks preparing quick snacks and light meals in a hurry, the pungency of fresh herbs delivers a great deal of aroma and flavor without recourse to lengthy cooking processes.

Left: Gruyère, Rosemary, and Tomato Toasties (page 22); right: Curried Eggs with Lemon-Parsley Sauce (page 26)

PINEAPPLE MINT
(Mentha
rotundifolia) *has a
very fruity tang. If it
is difficult to find, try
one of the many other
varieties of mint
with distinctive
flavors:* Applemint
(M. sauveolens)
*has a hint of
apples; eau de
cologne or orange
mint* (M. piperita
citrata) *has a very
sharp perfumed
scent and flavor;
ginger mint* (M.
gentilis) *is slightly
spicy.*

If PURPLE BASIL
(O. basilicum
*"Purpurascens") is
difficult to obtain,
you can use the
ordinary green
variety, although
the flavor will not
be quite the same.*

GRUYÈRE, ROSEMARY, AND TOMATO TOASTIES

MAKES 6

1 egg, lightly beaten
⅔ cup milk
salt and finely ground black pepper
3 slices of whole wheat bread
4 tbsp butter
2 tsp Dijon-style mustard
¾ cup shredded Gruyère or Swiss cheese
3 tomatoes, sliced
large sprig of fresh rosemary

Mix the egg with the milk in a shallow dish and season well. Remove the crusts from the bread and cut each slice across diagonally into 2 triangles. Soak these in the egg mixture.

Melt the butter in a frying pan over medium heat and fry the egg-coated bread slices until golden on both sides. Remove and place on paper towels to drain off excess fat.

Preheat the broiler.

Spread the top of each toasty thinly with mustard and then sprinkle with the cheese. Arrange the tomato slices on top and sprinkle spikes of rosemary over the tomato.

Place under the broiler and cook until the cheese begins to bubble.

PINEAPPLE MINT AND CUCUMBER MOUSSE

SERVES 4–6

piece of English cucumber, about 6½-inches long
1¼ cups cream cheese
2 tsp cider vinegar
1 tbsp minced fresh pineapple mint leaves
salt and freshly ground black pepper
2½ tsp unflavored gelatin
⅔ cup vegetable stock
crisp lettuce leaves, for serving
6 sprigs of pineapple mint, for garnish
toast triangles, for serving

Cut 12–18 thin slices of cucumber for garnish and reserve. Slice the rest thickly and put it in a blender or food processor with the cream cheese, vinegar, and mint. Process until smooth and then season.

In a small pan, dissolve the gelatin in 2 tablespoons of the stock over low heat. Let cool and then add this to the cheese mixture together with the remaining stock.

Blend once again until smooth. Adjust the seasoning, if necessary, and then place in a serving bowl. Cover and chill until set firmly, at least 1 hour.

Set the bowl on a bed of crisp lettuce and garnish with mint sprigs and the reserved cucumber slices. Serve with toast triangles.

RICOTTA, OLIVE, AND HERB RAMEKINS

SERVES 6

⅔ cup ricotta cheese
⅔ cup plain yogurt
5 tbsp butter, softened
2 garlic cloves, minced
1 tbsp each minced red and green
sweet pepper
3 tbsp pine nuts
1½ tbsp each minced black and green olives
1 tbsp minced fresh purple basil leaves
1 tbsp minced fresh flat-leaf parsley
salt and freshly ground black pepper
½ cucumber, peeled and thinly sliced, for garnish
strips of purple basil leaves, for garnish

Line 6 ramekin dishes with plastic wrap, leaving a large overhang all around so the dish can be covered.

Put the ricotta, yogurt, butter, and garlic in a bowl and mix them thoroughly. Add the peppers, pine nuts, olives, basil, parsley, and seasoning. Stir again to mix well.

Put the mixture in the lined dishes and smooth the tops. Cover with the overhanging wrap and chill overnight.

Unwrap the top of each ramekin, invert it to unmold, and remove the plastic wrap. Garnish each with overlapping cucumber slices and basil strips and serve.

Top: Pineapple Mint and Cucumber Mousse; bottom:
Ricotta, Olive, and Herb Ramekins

Any blue cheese can be used in the recipe for HERBED BOUCHÉES WITH BLUE CHEESE CREAM, *but Roquefort gives the finest results. "Bouchée" is French for "mouthful" and has become associated with these little pastries.*

CRUNCHY BEANS WITH LIME AND CILANTRO

SERVES 4

1 lb fine green beans
2 tbsp butter
juice of 1 lime
salt and freshly ground black pepper
1 tbsp minced fresh cilantro
slices of buttered sunflower-seed bread, for serving

Bring a large pan of water to a boil and add some salt and the beans. Keeping the water boiling, cook the beans until just crunchy, 3–5 minutes depending on size. Immediately drain, refresh under cold running water, and drain again.

Melt the butter in a heavy pan over heat and add half the lime juice. Add the drained beans and toss them to coat thoroughly in the butter and lime juice. Season, add half the cilantro and toss again.

Turn the contents of the pan into a warmed serving bowl. Squeeze the remaining lime juice over and sprinkle with the remaining cilantro. Serve immediately with the buttered bread.

HERBED BOUCHÉES WITH BLUE CHEESE CREAM

MAKES ABOUT 28

2 lb cold puff pastry
2 tsp herbes de Provence
2 eggs, beaten
4 oz blue cheese
¼ cup cream cheese
1 tbsp minced fresh parsley

Preheat the oven to 425°F.

Roll out the pastry to a thick rectangle. Sprinkle the herbs uniformly over the pastry and roll them in well. The pastry should end up about ¼-inch thick.

Using a 2-inch cookie cutter, cut out as many disks of pastry as possible, re-rolling trimmings as necessary. Using a 1-inch round cutter, make a cut in the center of each disk about halfway through the pastry, to make "lids."

Place the pastry disks on a baking sheet. Using a pastry brush, coat them lightly with the beaten egg. Bake until puffed and golden brown, 10–12 minutes.

While still warm, use the tip of a sharp knife to pry off the "lids" and reserve them.

In a bowl, mix the cheeses and the parsley together thoroughly. Using two teaspoons, fill the bouchées with this mixture.

Place the filled bouchées back in the oven for a few minutes to heat them through. Transfer to a warm serving platter, place the "lids" back on, and serve immediately.

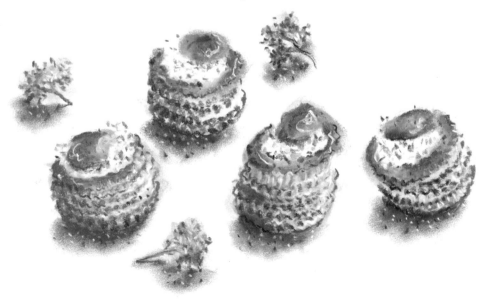

ZAHTAR

SERVES 4–6

½ cup walnut pieces
½ cup hazelnuts
¾ cup toasted sesame seeds
3 tbsp cumin seeds
¼ cup coriander seeds
sprig of fresh thyme
½ tsp salt
½ tsp crushed black peppercorns
¼ cup extra virgin olive oil
6 thick slices of brown bread, for serving

Using the slow pulse of a food processor, crush all the nuts and seeds with the thyme to fine crumbs – but be careful not to over-process. Transfer to a serving bowl and stir in the salt and pepper.

Place the olive oil in another small serving bowl. Remove the crusts from all but one end of each slice of bread and cut each slice into 4–6 fingers.

To serve: Dip the fingers of bread into the oil and then into the nut mixture.

CELERY ROOT RÉMOULADE WITH BERGAMOT

SERVES 4

1¼ cups mayonnaise
¼ lb celery root, finely shredded
1 onion, finely diced
1 tsp chopped capers
1 tsp chopped fresh chervil
1 tsp chopped fresh parsley
3 bergamot flowers
slices of crisp unleavened bread, for serving

Put the mayonnaise in a bowl, add the celery root, and mix thoroughly. Add the onion and capers,

then sprinkle in the herbs. Toss until well mixed.

Tear off the petals from one of the flowers and add these to the mixture. Cover with plastic wrap and chill 2 hours.

Uncover and serve garnished with the 2 remaining bergamot flowers. Serve with slices of crisp unleavened bread.

STUFFED SNOW PEAS

SERVES 4–6

36 snow peas (see below)
¼ cup crème fraîche or sour cream
1 tbsp minced fresh dill
2 tbsp cream cheese
grated zest and juice of 1 washed lime
salt and freshly ground black pepper
2 oz salmon or lumpfish caviar
radicchio or red lettuce leaves, for serving

Try to buy snow peas of a uniform size. Blanch them in boiling salted water 2 minutes. Immediately drain, refresh under cold water, drain again, and pat dry.

Using a sharp knife, slit the peas down one long side and open them carefully.

Put the crème fraîche in a bowl and mix in the dill and cream cheese. Add the zest and lime juice and seasoning, then gently fold in the caviar.

Use this mixture to stuff the snow peas and serve immediately on a bed of colorful leaves.

ZAHTAR *is an aromatic mixture popular in many Arab nations. It is sprinkled on food as a condiment, spread on bread, or used as a dip. In some places it is sold by street traders in small paper bags.*

CURRIED EGGS WITH LEMON-PARSLEY SAUCE★

SERVES 6

6 hard-cooked eggs, shelled and halved
½ tsp curry powder
2 tbsp whipping cream
½ tbsp minced fresh dill
1 large onion, minced
salt and freshly ground black pepper
2 oz salmon or lumpfish caviar
6 small parsley sprigs, for garnish
FOR THE LEMON-PARSLEY SAUCE
2 egg yolks
(★see page 2 for advice on eggs)
1 stick (8 tbsp) unsalted butter
1 tbsp minced fresh parsley
juice of ½ lemon

Carefully remove the yolks from the egg halves. Place the yolks in a bowl with the curry powder, cream, dill, and onion. Mix thoroughly and season. Fill the cavities in the egg halves with the mixture.

Make the lemon-parsley sauce: Put the egg yolks in a double boiler placed over low heat. Keep the water in the bottom pan at a constant simmer.

Using a wooden spoon, beat the egg yolks until they begin to thicken, 2–3 minutes. Add the butter, a few small pieces at a time, beating constantly.

When all the butter has been incorporated, add the parsley and lemon juice. Season and remove from the heat.

Spoon the sauce into the middle of 6 plates. Using a circular movement, tilt the plates so the sauce spreads out evenly.

Place 2 egg halves in the middle of the pool of sauce on each plate, spoon the caviar over them, and garnish with the parsley sprigs.

HERRING WITH FENNEL AND RED ONION

SERVES 4

8 small herrings, cleaned and heads removed
1 fennel bulb, thinly sliced
2 red onions, thinly sliced and separated into rings
salt and freshly ground black pepper
2 whole cloves
4 bay leaves
8 allspice berries
8 green peppercorns
½ cup tarragon vinegar
sprigs of fresh bay, for garnish

Remove the backbone from the fish by running the back of a spoon on the skin side from the tail to the head while exerting firm pressure. The backbone should then lift out quite cleanly.

Remove any stray bones and rinse the fish under cold running water. Pat dry, then lay flat on a clean surface with the flesh side uppermost. Arrange the slices of fennel and the onion rings in the center of the fish. Season and roll up the fish from the head to the tail. Secure with wooden toothpicks.

Place the rolled fish in a large heavy pan together with the cloves, bay leaves, allspice, green peppercorns, 1 teaspoon of salt, and some pepper. Pour the vinegar over the fish, then add just enough water to cover them.

Cover the pan, bring just to a boil, and simmer very gently until the flesh flakes easily when forked, 45–60 minutes.

Carefully transfer the fish to a deep serving dish and strain enough liquid over them to cover. Let cool completely, then cover and chill overnight.

Uncover and garnish the jellied fish with sprigs of fresh bay. Serve immediately before the jelly begins to melt.

CEVICHE

SERVES 4

2 whole mackerel, cleaned, or 4 skinned mackerel fillets
⅓ cup lime juice
⅓ cup lemon juice
salt and freshly ground black pepper
3 tbsp extra virgin olive oil
1 tbsp red wine vinegar
1 large onion, minced
1 tsp chopped fresh coriander (cilantro)
2 tbsp chopped fresh flat-leaf parsley
1 fresh hot chili pepper, seeded and finely chopped
2 large tomatoes, peeled and chopped
1 ripe avocado
tortilla chips, for serving

If using whole fish, press out the backbone of each and remove. Cut the fish or the fillets into chunks about ½-inch across.

Place the pieces of fish in a shallow dish and pour over the lime and lemon juices. Season, cover, and let marinate 6 hours, turning once or twice.

Put the oil, vinegar, onion, coriander, parsley, chili, and tomatoes in another bowl and mix together thoroughly.

Drain the fish, reserving the juice. Mix the fish with the herb and tomato mixture and transfer to a serving dish.

Halve and pit the avocado. Peel and slice the flesh thinly, then arrange the slices on top of the fish mixture. Using a pastry brush, coat the avocado with the reserved juice to prevent discoloration.

Season with salt and pepper and serve with tortilla chips.

Top: Smoked Trout and Dill in Whitefish Cornets; bottom: Ceviche

SMOKED MACKEREL PÂTÉ WITH HORSERADISH

SERVES 4

4 smoked mackerel fillets, skinned
2 tbsp butter, softened
⅔ cup light cream
3 tbsp coarsely chopped hazelnuts
1 tbsp lime juice
1 tbsp cream-style horseradish
salt and freshly ground black pepper
slices of warm toast, for serving

Put all the ingredients into a blender or food processor with some seasoning. Process until smooth, then transfer to a bowl. Serve with toast.

SMOKED TROUT AND DILL IN WHITEFISH CORNETS

SERVES 4

6 oz smoked trout fillets, skinned and flaked
1 tbsp minced fresh dill
1 tbsp cream-style horseradish
salt and freshly ground black pepper
¾ lb very thin slices of smoked whitefish
2 slices of whole wheat toast
small bunch of fresh chervil
juice of ½ lemon and 1 lime

Place the smoked trout, dill, and horseradish in a small bowl. Season and mix together thoroughly.

Lay the whitefish slices on a flat surface and cut them into 8 strips. Spread each piece with the smoked trout mixture, then roll up into a cornet.

Cut each slice of toast into 4 rectangles. Place on a serving platter, then sit the cornets on top of them.

Garnish with chervil. Dribble the fruit juices over and sprinkle with pepper just before serving.

CEVICHE *is a dish native to South America in which raw fish "cooks" in a lime juice marinade.*

You can substitute SMOKED SALMON *or* SMOKED EEL *for the Whitefish.*

MAIN COURSES

W hen preparing main courses using herbs, all the classic time-honored associations come to the fore . . . lamb with rosemary, fish with dill, chicken with tarragon, and so on. However, slightly more adventurous combinations, like my *Sautéed Lamb with Fennel Sauce*, can be very rewarding. When preparing a roast, for example, if in doubt add the herb only at the last minute to a little of the gravy to make sure it is to your taste. If so, then next time spike the meat with the herb at an early stage or even marinate it. Herbs also have the power to transform fairly humble ingredients into impressive meals, for instance in the recipe for *Pork Chops with Apple and Juniper*.

From left to right: Venison and Sage Patties with Pears (page 40), Roast Pheasant with Thyme-Brandy Cream (page 39) and Pork Chops with Apple and Juniper (page 39)

SEAFOOD IN HERB AND SAFFRON SAUCE

SERVES 4

3 tbsp olive oil
1 onion, chopped
1 red sweet pepper, seeded and sliced
1 green sweet pepper, seeded and sliced
2 large garlic cloves, minced
2 tsp paprika
¼ lb prepared squid, coarsely chopped
4 tomatoes, peeled and coarsely chopped
½ tsp ground saffron
2 bay leaves
1 cup sliced almonds
¾ cup dry white wine
grated zest and juice of 1 washed lime
1¼ cups fish stock
salt and freshly ground black pepper
¼ lb peeled and deveined medium or large shrimp
¼ lb shucked small hardshell clams
¼ lb sea scallops, halved if large
3 tbsp brandy
1 tbsp chopped fresh dill
½ cup light cream
fresh flat-leaf parsley, for garnish
hot crusty bread, for serving

Heat the oil in a large heavy pot over medium heat. Add the onion, peppers, garlic, paprika, and squid and sauté gently for 10 minutes.

Stir in the tomatoes, saffron, bay leaves, almonds, wine, lime zest and juice, and stock. Bring to a boil and simmer 3 minutes. Season.

Reduce the heat and add the shrimp, clams, and scallops. Mix thoroughly, cover, and simmer 5 minutes. Add the brandy and dill and simmer 3 minutes more. Stir in the cream and adjust the seasoning, if necessary. Garnish with parsley just before serving, with hot crusty bread.

SAFFRON, *the dried stamens of a type of crocus, is one of the most ancient and valued of spices. As well as imparting a wonderful golden color, it also gives a subtly strong flavor that works particularly well with fish and seafood, rice, and some pastries.*

SWEDISH FISH SOUFFLÉ WITH DILL

SERVES 4–6

7 tbsp butter, plus more for greasing
2 tbsp crisp bread crumbs
4 eggs, separated
⅔ cup flour
2½ cups milk
½ lb cooked finnan haddie, flaked
1 tbsp minced fresh dill
salt and freshly ground black pepper

Preheat the oven to 425°F and grease a 7-inch soufflé dish carefully with butter, making sure that the rim is also well coated. Then dust this layer of butter with the bread crumbs, shaking out any excess.

Beat the egg whites to stiff peaks.

Melt the butter in a large heavy saucepan over medium heat. Stir in the flour and cook gently 2 minutes. Slowly add the milk, stirring constantly. Reduce the heat and cook 5 minutes longer.

Remove from the heat and add the egg yolks, one at a time, followed by the fish. Stir a spoonful of the egg whites into this mixture to loosen it and then carefully fold in the remaining egg whites together with the dill and seasoning to taste.

Fill the prepared dish with the soufflé mixture and tap the dish on a work surface to help the mixture settle with a level top and no air pockets.

Set the dish in a roasting pan and pour boiling water into this to about halfway up the sides of the soufflé dish.

Bake until the soufflé is well risen and golden brown, 30–40 minutes. Serve immediately.

Left: Tuna Roulade with Dill and Capers (page 34); right: Seafood in Herb and Saffron Sauce

TUNA ROULADE WITH DILL AND CAPERS

SERVES 4–8

7 oz canned tuna in oil
4 eggs, separated
salt and freshly ground black pepper
2 tbsp freshly grated Parmesan cheese

FOR THE FILLING

1¼ cups milk
1 onion, quartered
2 large sprigs of parsley, minced
1 bay leaf
2 tbsp butter
3 tbsp flour
4 hard-cooked eggs, shelled and coarsely chopped
1 tsp grated zest and 1 tsp juice from a lemon
2 tbsp minced fresh dill
1 tsp capers

ROULADE *is the French term for rolled and stuffed items, especially used for meats and omelette mixtures, as with this* TUNA ROULADE. *Canned salmon makes a good alternative to tuna.*

Preheat the oven to 400°F and line a 13-×9-inch jelly roll pan with wax paper.

Prepare the filling: Pour the milk into a small pan and add the onion, parsley, and bay leaf. Bring quickly to a boil. Cover and let infuse off the heat at least 20 minutes.

Meanwhile, in a mixing bowl, mash the tuna with its oil to a purée using a hand blender or fork.

Beat the egg yolks lightly, then beat them into the tuna purée. Season. Beat the egg whites to stiff peaks and gently fold them into the tuna mixture.

Pour the mixture into the prepared pan and level with a spatula. Bake on the top shelf of the oven until well risen, firm, and light golden in color, 10–15 minutes. Let cool in the pan.

Finish the filling: Melt the butter in a saucepan over medium heat. Add the flour and stir 2 minutes. Add the strained milk, stirring constantly, and gently bring to a boil. Reduce the heat and simmer 3 minutes. Add the eggs, lemon zest and juice, dill, and capers. Season.

Sprinkle a piece of wax paper slightly larger than the jelly roll pan with the Parmesan cheese. Turn the cooled roulade out on the paper and peel off the lining paper from the base.

Reheat the filling, if necessary, and spread it over the roulade with a spatula, leaving a 1 inch clear border all the way around.

Lift one short end of the paper and roll up the roulade like a jelly roll. Transfer to a serving dish, sprinkle any remaining Parmesan on the top, and serve immediately, cut in thick slices.

GRILLED SALMON STEAKS WITH SAFFRON SAUCE

SERVES 4

4 salmon steaks, each weighing about 6 oz
FOR THE MARINADE
2 tbsp lime juice
1 tbsp honey
⅓ cup hazelnut oil
salt and freshly ground black pepper
FOR THE SAFFRON SAUCE
¼ tsp ground saffron
⅔ cup dry white wine
2 egg yolks
1¼ cups whipping cream
4 tbsp butter, cut into small chunks
1 tbsp lemon juice

Put the salmon steaks in a shallow dish. Mix together the marinade ingredients and season well. Pour this over the fish, cover, and let marinate in the refrigerator 12 hours, turning from time to time.

Make the saffron sauce: Dissolve the saffron in the wine in a small pan and heat gently, stirring constantly. Cover and simmer 3 minutes. Remove from the heat and let cool.

In a bowl, mix the egg yolks with the cream. Stir in the cooled wine and saffron mixture. Return this mixture to the pan and heat gently, stirring constantly, until it thickens. Do not let it boil. Remove from the heat but keep warm.

Preheat a hot grill. Drain the salmon steaks, pat them dry, and grill them about 4 minutes on each side.

While the steaks are cooking, strain the sauce. Then whisk in the butter, a little at a time, followed by the lemon juice and seasoning to taste.

Place the fish on a warmed serving platter, pour over the saffron sauce, and serve immediately.

SAUTÉED LAMB WITH FENNEL SAUCE

SERVES 6

2 tbsp walnut oil
2 lb boneless lamb loin or sirloin, cut into small pieces
½-inch thick
FOR THE FENNEL SAUCE
⅔ cup vegetable stock
2 fennel bulbs, thinly sliced, with the feathery leaves
reserved for garnish
2 tbsp butter
1 tbsp flour
1¼ cups light cream
salt and freshly ground black pepper

First make the sauce: Put the stock in a pan with the fennel. Cover, bring to a boil, and simmer 25 minutes over medium heat. Remove from the heat and let cool.

When cool, purée the mixture in a blender or food processor and then push through a fine strainer.

Melt the butter in a pan over medium heat, add the flour, and cook, stirring constantly, for 3 minutes.

Remove from the heat and stir in the fennel purée. Return to the heat and stir constantly for 5 minutes. Gradually add the cream and then season to taste.

Heat the walnut oil in a frying pan over medium heat and add the lamb slices. Sprinkle with salt and pepper, increase the heat, and sauté the lamb 3 minutes, stirring constantly.

Transfer the lamb to a warmed serving dish, cover with the fennel sauce, and garnish with the reserved fennel fronds.

NUT OILS, *such as those made by pressing walnuts and hazelnuts, have fine nutty flavors. Excellent in moderation in salad dressings, they are available from specialty stores and many supermarkets. Buy them in small quantities because a little goes a long way and they turn rancid quickly.*

HERBED LEG OF LAMB WITH TOMATO SAUCE

SERVES 6–8

1 boned lamb center-leg roast, weighing about 3 lb
3 small sprigs of fresh rosemary
½ tsp each snipped fresh basil, thyme, and oregano
sea salt and freshly ground black pepper
FOR THE SAUCE
1 tsp olive oil
2 onions, coarsely chopped
2 garlic cloves, minced
1 green sweet pepper, seeded and thinly sliced
1 red sweet pepper, seeded and thinly sliced
2 cups canned peeled tomatoes, drained
1 tbsp tomato paste
¼ lb oyster mushrooms, coarsely chopped
⅔ cup dry white wine

Preheat the oven to 450°F.

Lay the meat out flat and sprinkle it with the herbs and seasoning. Roll up as tightly as possible, then tie with string.

Place in a roasting pan and roast 25 minutes. Reduce the temperature to 425°F and roast 45–50 minutes longer. Transfer to a warmed serving platter and keep warm.

Make the sauce: Put the olive oil in a heavy pan over medium heat, add the onions and garlic, and sauté until translucent, 3–5 minutes.

Add the peppers and combine thoroughly with the onions. Cook 2 minutes, then add the tomatoes, tomato paste, and mushrooms. Stir well and cook 2 minutes longer.

Season and add the wine. Increase the heat and bring to a boil, stirring constantly. Continue to boil to reduce a little, then serve with the lamb.

Left: Herbed Leg of Lamb with Tomato Sauce; Broccoli and Cauliflower with Five-Herb Butter (page 45)

CHICKEN BAKED WITH SAVORY AND ORANGE

SERVES 4

1 tbsp freshly grated peeled gingerroot
½ tsp ground cloves
¾ tsp coarse salt
1 tsp coarsely ground black pepper
½ tsp ground coriander seeds
8 sprigs of fresh winter savory
3 tbsp butter, softened
1 large chicken, cut into quarters
1½ tbsp orange juice
thinly pared zest from 1 washed orange, cut into julienne strips
¾ cup dry white wine

Preheat the oven to 400°F.

Place the ginger, cloves, salt, black pepper, coriander seeds, and 2 sprigs of winter savory in a blender or food processor and process until fine. In a bowl, blend this mixture into the softened butter.

Lift the skin gently from the chicken quarters and make several incisions in the meat. Fill the incisions with the butter mixture, then replace the skin, securing with wooden toothpicks.

Line a baking dish with foil and place the remaining winter savory sprigs in the dish. Put the chicken on top of the savory and pour over the orange juice.

Bake until tender and the juices run clear when a skewer is inserted in the thickest part of the thigh, 40–50 minutes. Transfer the chicken to a warmed serving platter and keep warm.

Place the orange zest strips in a small pan and add the wine. Cover and simmer 3 minutes. Add the juices and the savory from the baking dish and bring to a boil. Boil 2 minutes to reduce slightly.

Strain the sauce into a warmed gravy boat and serve with the chicken.

A wide variety of herbs will work in the HERBED LEG OF LAMB. *The traditional mint or parsley goes especially well.*

CHICKEN BREASTS WITH COCONUT-TARRAGON CREAM

SERVES 4

3 tbsp butter
1 tbsp hazelnut oil
2 tbsp chopped fresh tarragon
4 large boneless chicken breast halves
2 tbsp canned unsweetened coconut cream
salt and freshly ground black pepper

Melt the butter with the oil in a heavy pan over medium heat. Add half the tarragon, followed by the chicken breasts. Cover and cook about 5 minutes.

Remove the lid and turn the chicken breasts over. Season, increase the heat a little, and cook 5 minutes longer.

Reduce the heat to medium and add the coconut cream. Baste the chicken and adjust the seasoning, if necessary.

Increase the heat again, turn the breasts once more, and cook 2 minutes longer.

Transfer the chicken and its sauce to a warmed serving platter and garnish with the remaining tarragon.

Note: This dish works equally well with more economical pieces of chicken such as drumsticks, thighs, or wings.

Left: Falafel (page 41); right: Chicken Breasts with Coconut-Tarragon Cream

ROAST PHEASANT WITH THYME-BRANDY CREAM

SERVES 4–6

2 large young pheasants
2 washed oranges, quartered
2 washed lemons, quartered
5 tbsp butter
6 thin slices of bacon
1 tbsp hazelnut oil
4 onions, chopped
4 bay leaves
2 large sprigs of fresh thyme
2 tbsp brandy
1 1/4 cups whipping cream
salt and freshly ground black pepper
large bunch of watercress, for garnish

Preheat the oven to 450°F.

Wipe the pheasants thoroughly inside and out and stuff the cavities with alternating orange and lemon quarters.

Place the pheasants in a roasting pan and smooth 2 tablespoons of the butter over each bird, using a spatula. Cover the breasts with the bacon. Season and pour 2/3 cup of water into the pan.

Place on the middle shelf of the oven and roast 45 minutes, basting frequently with the pan juices.

Toward the end of this time, melt the remaining butter with the hazelnut oil in a saucepan over medium heat. Add the onions and sauté gently until translucent. Add the bay leaves and sprinkle the thyme into the onions. Cover and simmer 5 minutes.

When the pheasants are cooked, use a spoon to squash the oranges and lemons in the birds' cavities, then drain the juice into the pan. Remove and discard the citrus quarters, place the pheasants on a warmed serving platter, and keep hot.

Add the roasting pan juices to the onion mixture and increase the heat. Warm the brandy in a small pan over very low heat and add it to the sauce. Then gently stir in the cream, taking care that it does not boil. Adjust the seasoning, if necessary, and transfer to a warmed gravy boat.

Serve the carved birds garnished with watercress accompanied by the sauce.

PORK CHOPS WITH APPLE AND JUNIPER

SERVES 4

4 or 8 large center-cut pork chops
2 1/2 cups buttermilk
8 juniper berries, crushed
salt and freshly ground black pepper
6 crab apples or tart red apples, unpeeled, cored, and sliced
1/2 tbsp cornstarch

In a shallow dish, marinate the chops in the buttermilk for 36 hours.

Preheat a hot grill. Remove the chops and reserve the buttermilk. Pat the meat dry. Mix the juniper berries with salt and pepper and press this mixture on both sides of the pieces of meat. Grill for 5–10 minutes on each side, until cooked as desired.

While the chops are broiling, put the buttermilk in a heavy saucepan and add the apple slices. Bring to a boil and simmer gently for 5 minutes.

In a small bowl, combine 2 tablespoons of the buttermilk with the cornstarch and mix thoroughly. Add this to the buttermilk and apple mixture and bring to a boil, stirring constantly. Reduce the heat and simmer gently for 3 minutes, still stirring. Season. Serve this sauce immediately to accompany the pork chops.

GUINEA FOWL *can be substituted for pheasant. Its slightly game-like flavor is enhanced by the rich sauce.*

VENISON *is available from good butchers, specialty stores, and some supermarkets. The meat of wild deer has an incomparable flavor. Nowadays, however, most venison is farm-raised and as a result is less expensive – but inferior in flavor to wild meat.*

RABBIT CASSEROLE WITH MUSTARD AND MARJORAM

SERVES 6

½ cup vegetable oil
1 rabbit, weighing about 2¼–3 lb, cut into pieces
2 tbsp Dijon-style mustard
¼ cup flour
2 tbsp tomato paste
3 bay leaves
1 tsp dried marjoram
1¼ cups vegetable stock
1¼ cups red wine
2 garlic cloves, minced
salt and freshly ground black pepper
½ lb thin slices of bacon
4 slices of whole wheat bread, for garnish

Preheat the oven to 350°F.

Heat half the oil in a deep sauté pan over medium heat and brown the pieces of rabbit on all sides.

Using a slotted spoon, transfer the browned rabbit pieces to a large casserole dish. Using a spatula, spread them with the mustard.

Add the flour and tomato paste to the oil in the sauté pan and cook 2 minutes, stirring constantly. Add the herbs, stock, and wine, followed by the garlic. Season with 1 teaspoon of salt and some pepper. Bring to a boil and simmer 2 minutes.

Pour the sauce over the rabbit, cover the casserole, and cook in the oven for 2½ hours.

Roll up the bacon slices, then halve these rolls. Skewer them with wooden toothpicks and fry them until well browned. Add them to the casserole 30 minutes before the end of the cooking time.

About 10 minutes before the end of the cooking time, cut each slice of bread into 4 triangles. Heat the remaining oil in a frying pan until very hot and fry the bread triangles until golden brown. Drain.

Adjust the seasoning of the casserole, if necessary, and serve garnished with the bread croûtes.

VENISON AND SAGE PATTIES WITH PEARS

SERVES 6

1½ lb ground venison
1 tbsp grated zest and 3 tbsp juice from 1 washed lemon
½ tbsp minced fresh sage
1 bay leaf, finely minced
½ tbsp chopped fresh parsley
salt and freshly ground black pepper
12 thin slices of bacon
6 fresh pears, peeled, sliced, and warmed

Mix the venison, lemon zest and juice, sage, bay leaf, and parsley in a bowl. Cover and let marinate 24 hours.

Preheat the broiler or a charcoal grill.

Season the marinated mixture and form it into 6 patties. Wrap 2 slices of bacon around each one and secure with wooden toothpicks. Broil or grill 6 minutes on each side.

Place on a warmed serving platter and arrange the warmed pear slices decoratively on top before serving.

ZUCCHINI, TOMATO, AND GARLIC FLAN

SERVES 4

butter, for greasing
pie pastry made with 1 cup flour, 6 tbsp shortening,
and 2 tbsp ice water
¾ lb zucchini
2 eggs, beaten
⅔ cup milk
⅔ cup whipping cream
2 garlic cloves, minced
1 tsp tomato paste
1 tsp Worcestershire sauce
¼ tsp freshly grated nutmeg
salt and freshly ground black pepper
¼ lb tomatoes, sliced

Preheat the oven to 400°F and grease a 7-inch loose-bottomed tart or quiche pan with some butter.

Roll out the pastry and use it to line the pan. Line with wax paper and weight with some dried beans. Bake 15 minutes. Let cool and then remove the beans and lining paper.

Grate the zucchini and blanch the shreds 30 seconds only in boiling salted water. Drain, refresh under cold running water, and set aside.

In a bowl, thoroughly mix the eggs, milk, cream, garlic, tomato paste, Worcestershire sauce, nutmeg, and seasoning. Add the well-drained zucchini and spread this mixture evenly in the pastry shell. Arrange the tomatoes decoratively on the top.

Bake until set and golden, 30–40 minutes.

FALAFEL

MAKES 14–16

2⅓ cups cooked but firm chickpeas (garbanzos)
2 onions, minced
½ tsp turmeric
½ tsp cayenne pepper
1 tsp ground coriander seeds
1 tsp ground cumin
2 garlic cloves, minced
1 tbsp whole wheat flour
2 tbsp whole wheat bread crumbs
½ tsp baking powder
salt and freshly ground black pepper
more whole wheat flour, for dusting (optional)
vegetable oil, for deep-frying

Place the chickpeas, onions, spices, garlic, flour, bread crumbs, baking powder, and seasoning in a blender or food processor and pulse gently until thoroughly mixed. Cover and let rest 45 minutes.

Shape the mixture into balls (if too sticky, roll lightly in whole wheat flour).

Put the oil in a deep pan and heat to 385°F (a small cube of dry bread will brown in 20 seconds). Deep-fry the balls, a few at a time, removing and draining each batch on paper towels when they are golden brown. Keep warm on a warmed serving dish until all are cooked.

Serve accompanied by a tomato salad.

FALAFEL are rissoles made from spiced purées of beans or chickpeas. Egyptian in origin, they are now popular throughout the Middle East. Being high in protein, they are a favorite dish with vegetarians.

VEGETABLES AND SALADS

*I*t is in the preparation of vegetables and salads that most fresh herbs really come into their own. As well as marrying their flavors wonderfully well with those of the other ingredients, many have the power to bring out the basic flavor of the other vegetables and leaves. Moreover, a simple herb butter, mayonnaise, or sauce can transform a plainly boiled or steamed vegetable from a humdrum accompaniment into a glorious feast in its own right. In salads, fresh herbs can be enjoyed for their texture as well as their taste. Salads are also the perfect place to use herb flowers, for both their interesting flavors and their very decorative appearance. Pour dressing over flowers only at the very last minutes, if at all, or they will discolor.

Left: Baked Beets with Horseradish Cream (page 44); right: Green and White Bean Salad with Mint (page 44)

BAKED BEETS WITH HORSERADISH CREAM

SERVES 4

4 large beets
1 tbsp cream-style horseradish
2 tbsp light cream
salt and freshly ground black pepper

Preheat the oven to 400°F.

Wash the beets gently, trying not to bruise their skins. Leave the root and stem intact if possible. Place them in a foil-lined baking pan and bake until soft all the way through, 50–60 minutes.

Gently lift the beets from the pan, cut off the root ends, and halve the beets. Place the 2 halves of each beet cut-side up on each of 4 warmed plates.

Mix the horseradish and cream. Season and serve cold with the hot beets. Alternatively, warm the mixture in a double boiler and serve hot.

BAKED BEETS WITH HORSERADISH CREAM *makes an excellent first course.*

The FIVE-HERB BUTTER *works equally well with most vegetables, especially new potatoes and leeks, and is delicious with steaks and fish.*

GREEN AND WHITE BEAN SALAD WITH MINT

SERVES 4

1 cup dried flageolet beans, soaked overnight
1 cup dried navy beans, soaked overnight
1 large zucchini, thinly sliced
1 large onion, thinly sliced
1 large green sweet pepper, seeded and coarsely chopped
1 large red sweet pepper, seeded and coarsely chopped
2 large tomatoes, seeded and coarsely chopped
4 garlic cloves, minced
1 tbsp coarsely snipped fresh mint
1 tbsp minced fresh parsley
grated zest of 1 washed lemon
7 tbsp extra virgin olive oil
2 tbsp white wine vinegar
salt and freshly ground black pepper

Drain the beans, cover them with fresh cold water, and bring it to a boil. Drain and repeat the process. When boiling for the second time, cover, reduce the heat, and simmer until the beans are tender, about 1 hour. Add more water from time to time, as necessary.

Drain the beans and refresh under cold running water. When thoroughly drained, place them in a salad bowl. Add the other ingredients except the oil and vinegar. Toss gently to mix well.

Mix the oil and vinegar and season to taste. Pour this over the salad and toss again before serving.

BROCCOLI AND CAULIFLOWER WITH FIVE-HERB BUTTER

SERVES 4–6

½ lb broccoli florets
½ lb cauliflower florets
salt
FOR THE HERB BUTTER
1 stick (8 tbsp) butter
½ tsp each minced fresh marjoram, mint, chives,
and tarragon
1 tsp minced fresh parsley
1 tbsp lemon juice

Several hours before, make the herb butter: Cream the butter in a bowl until light. Gently work in the herbs and lemon juice. Leave at room temperature about 2 hours to let the herbs release their flavors and then chill 1–2 hours.

Blanch the broccoli and cauliflower florets in boiling salted water 3–5 minutes, depending on the desired degree of crunchiness.

Using a wire skimmer or slotted spoon, transfer the vegetables to a colander and refresh under cold water. Then return the florets to the boiling water for 1 minute only to reheat.

Transfer to a warmed serving dish, dot with herb butter, and serve immediately.

HUNGARIAN SQUASH

SERVES 4

*1–1 ½ lb summer squash such as vegetable marrow,
crookneck, or patty pan
5 tbsp butter
1 onion
½ tsp caraway seeds
3 tbsp white wine vinegar
2 tsp paprika
½ tsp sugar
½ cup light cream
1 tsp minced fresh dill
salt and freshly ground black pepper*

For a spicier version of HUNGARIAN SQUASH, *try using cayenne to taste instead of paprika.*

Peel the squash, and cut it into quarters, scoop out and discard the seeds, and slice the flesh thinly.

Melt the butter in a large pan over high heat, add the squash slices, and cook quickly 5 minutes, turning constantly. Remove the squash from the pan and keep warm.

Place the onion and caraway seeds in the pan and cook 2 minutes. Add the vinegar and paprika and cook 5 minutes longer over medium heat. Add the sugar and stir until it is completely dissolved.

Reduce the heat, then add the cream followed by the squash and the dill, stirring to coat evenly. Cover and cook gently for 3 minutes over very low heat, taking care that it does not boil.

Adjust the seasoning and serve in a warmed dish.

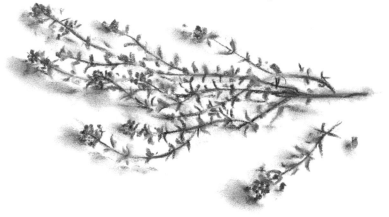

TOMATO, THYME, AND SPINACH TARTLETS

MAKES 18

*4 tbsp butter, plus more for greasing
pie pastry made with 3 cups flour (half whole wheat
and half all-purpose), 1 cup + 2 tbsp shortening,
and about ½ cup ice water
2 onions, thinly sliced
1 tsp dried thyme
1 cup freshly grated Parmesan cheese
⅓ cup puréed cooked spinach
1 tbsp Dijon-style mustard
4 eggs, beaten
½ cup crème fraîche or whipping cream
salt and freshly ground black pepper
6 small tomatoes, thinly sliced*

Preheat the oven to 350°F and grease 18 small tartlet molds with butter.

On a cold surface, roll out the pastry to a thickness of about ⅛ inch. Use to line the prepared molds, re-rolling the trimmings, if necessary. Cover and chill.

Melt the butter in a pan over low heat, add the onions, and sauté until translucent, about 6 minutes, adding the thyme halfway through. Remove from the heat and let cool.

Spoon this mixture into the tartlet shells, then sprinkle with half the Parmesan. Do not over-fill.

In a bowl, combine the remaining ingredients, except the tomatoes. Season the mixture and pour it into the tartlet shells.

Arrange the tomato slices on the top, sprinkle over the remaining Parmesan, and bake until the filling is set and golden, 15–20 minutes.

Left: Tomato, Thyme, and Spinach Tartlets; right: Crisp, Bacon, Bean, and Parsley Salad (page 51)

TOMATO, THYME, AND SPINACH TARTLETS *make excellent accompaniments to any dish of legumes. Made in four larger tartlet molds, they can also be served as appetizers, snacks, or picnic food.*

VEGETARIAN TORTA WITH SAGE HOLLANDAISE★

SERVES 6

3 tbsp hazelnut oil, plus more for greasing
2 onions, coarsely chopped
6 Roma tomatoes, coarsely chopped
¼ lb oyster mushrooms, coarsely chopped
1 tsp herbes de Provence
1 tbsp light soy sauce
nearly ½ cup buckwheat groats
2½ tbsp brown rice
1 egg, beaten
⅔ cup vegetable stock
freshly ground black pepper
1 tbsp crushed hazelnuts
2 large fresh sage leaves, for garnish

FOR THE GOLDEN SAGE HOLLANDAISE SAUCE

1 tbsp finely snipped fresh golden sage
2 tbsp lemon juice
1 tbsp white wine vinegar
14 tbsp unsalted butter
3 egg yolks
(★see page 2 for advice on eggs)
1 tbsp dry white wine
salt and freshly ground black pepper

The SAGE
HOLLANDAISE
sauce also goes very
well with chicken
and veal and with
rice, cheese, and
tomato dishes.

Preheat the oven to 375°F and lightly grease a 7-inch-long shallow loaf pan with a little hazelnut oil.

Heat the hazelnut oil in a pan over medium heat. Add the onions, tomatoes, and mushrooms, toss gently to coat evenly, and cook 3 minutes. Add the herbs and the soy sauce and cook 2 minutes longer. Add the buckwheat and rice and cook 2 minutes more. Then stir in the egg.

Add the vegetable stock and bring to a boil, stirring constantly. Reduce the heat, cover, and simmer until all the liquid has been absorbed, 20–25 minutes. Season with pepper and add the hazelnuts.

Transfer the mixture to the prepared pan and bake 45 minutes.

Meanwhile, make the hollandaise sauce: Mix the chopped sage with 1 tablespoon of the lemon juice, the vinegar, and 1 tablespoon of water in a small pan and bring to a boil. Drain the sage in a strainer and set it aside. Melt 12 tablespoons of the butter in the top pan of a double boiler over very low heat. Transfer to a warmed measuring cup.

Place the egg yolks in the double boiler and beat them quickly with a whisk. Add half the remaining lemon juice and all the wine together with a pinch of salt. Beat again. Add half the remaining unmelted butter and place the pan over the bottom pan of the double boiler.

Whisking steadily, cook gently until the egg yolks are creamy and beginning to thicken. Immediately remove the pan from the heat and stir in the remaining unmelted butter until evenly blended.

Dribble the melted butter into the yolk mixture, whisking fast. Add the butter more rapidly as the sauce thickens. When the sauce is the consistency of whipping cream, add the remaining lemon juice with the reserved sage and adjust the seasoning.

Serve the sauce with the hot vegetarian torta garnished with the whole sage leaves.

GRAPE LEAVES STUFFED WITH CILANTRO RICE

SERVES 4–6

½ lb grape preserved leaves or 40 fresh leaves
2¾ cups cooked brown rice
2 tbsp tomato paste
2 onions, diced
2 garlic cloves, minced
1 tsp ground cinnamon
2 tbsp minced fresh cilantro
1 tbsp currants
1 tbsp sliced almonds
salt and freshly ground black pepper
2 tbsp walnut oil
juice of 2 limes
2 cups vegetable stock

Place the fresh grape leaves in a large bowl and scald them thoroughly with boiling water. If using preserved leaves, let them soak 10 minutes.

Drain the leaves, refresh under cold water, and lay flat on paper towels, dull-side up.

In a bowl, combine the rice, tomato paste, onions, garlic, cinnamon, cilantro, currants, almonds, and seasoning.

Place 10 leaves in the bottom of a Dutch oven. Cut any stems from the other leaves and place a scant tablespoon of the filling in the center of each leaf. Fold the stem end of the leaf over the filling, then fold in the sides and continue to roll up the leaf carefully from the stem end to form a firm package about 2-inches long.

Place these side by side, seam side down, in the Dutch oven. Sprinkle with the walnut oil and lime juice, and add just enough vegetable stock to cover them. If necessary, add a little water.

Cover the pot and bring to a gentle simmer. Simmer over low heat about 1 hour. Throughout this time check that the grape leaves remain moist.

Transfer to a warmed serving dish and serve any excess liquid as a sauce.

If serving cold, let cool in the covered pot, then transfer to a serving dish.

If GRAPE LEAVES are difficult to obtain, use large spinach or Swiss chard leaves. The rice stuffing can also be flavored with ground lamb or chicken.

WATERCRESS, MANDARIN, AND PRIMROSE SALAD

SERVES 4

2 bunches of watercress
¼ lb lamb's lettuce
½ cup canned mandarins in juice, drained
½ washed orange
¾ tbsp Dijon-style mustard
3 tbsp light vegetable oil
2 tbsp white wine vinegar
1 tbsp fresh orange juice
1 tsp minced fresh tarragon
salt and freshly ground black pepper
2 tsp minced primrose leaves
4 primrose flower heads, for garnish (optional)

Mix the watercress and lamb's lettuce in a salad bowl. Arrange the mandarin sections over the salad.

Peel the orange, discarding as much pith as possible. Slice the flesh thinly and cut the zest into fine julienne strips. Add these to the salad.

Combine the mustard, oil, vinegar, orange juice, and tarragon in a screw-top jar. Shake vigorously, then season.

Shake the jar again well before dressing the salad. Arrange the chopped primrose leaves on the salad and serve.

Toss again at the table and garnish with the whole primrose flower heads, if using.

CRISP BACON, BEAN, AND PARSLEY SALAD

SERVES 4

3 cups canned lima beans, drained
6 slices of bacon
10 dried apricots, sliced into thin slivers
3 tbsp coarsely chopped hazelnuts
1½ tbsp coarsely chopped fresh parsley
6 tbsp olive oil
2 tbsp wine vinegar
¾ tbsp coarse-grain mustard
salt and freshly ground black pepper

Rinse the beans under cold running water, drain, and dry on paper towels.

Fry the bacon over medium-high heat until crisp. Drain on paper towels to remove excess fat. Crumble the cooked bacon coarsely into pieces.

Place the beans in a salad bowl. Add the bacon, apricots, hazelnuts, and parsley and toss well.

Pour the oil and vinegar into a screw-top jar. Add the mustard and shake vigorously. Season with salt and pepper and shake again. Pour over the salad and toss well to serve.

The flowers and leaves of all varieties of PRIMROSE *are edible.*

Left: Vegetarian Torta with Sage Hollandaise (page 48);
right: Watercress, Mandarin, and Primrose Salad

Tamari sauce is a fine Japanese soy sauce made by fermentation. If unobtainable, use a good light soy sauce. If Japanese rice vinegar is difficult to obtain, use light cider vinegar.

Tahini paste, made from crushed sesame seeds, is a common Middle-Eastern condiment. It is available from many supermarkets.

ZUCCHINI AND PURPLE BASIL SALAD

SERVES 4–6

1½ lb zucchini, coarsely grated
3 tomatoes, coarsely chopped
2 onions, thinly sliced
1 tbsp poppy seeds
2 tbsp extra virgin olive oil
1 tbsp finely snipped fresh purple basil leaves
1 tbsp tamari sauce
1 tbsp Japanese rice vinegar
freshly ground black pepper

Put the zucchini, tomatoes, onions, and poppy seeds in a salad bowl and gently mix.

Put the oil, basil, tamari, rice vinegar, and pepper in a screw-top jar and shake vigorously. Dress the salad with the mixture, toss well, and serve.

CHICKEN SALAD WITH SESAME-CUCUMBER SAUCE

SERVES 4–6

3 skinless boneless chicken breast halves
1 tbsp freshly grated peeled gingerroot
4 scallions, including the green tops
2 small English cucumbers
1 head of Iceberg lettuce, for serving
FOR THE SESAME-CUCUMBER SAUCE
1 tsp peanut oil
1 tsp chili oil
¼ tsp dry mustard
1 tbsp light soy sauce
2 tbsp tahini paste
1 tbsp rice vinegar
2 tbsp water
salt and freshly ground black pepper
1 tbsp minced green scallion tops
1 tbsp toasted sesame seeds

Place the chicken breasts in a pan with the ginger, scallions, and 3 cups of water and bring to a boil. Cover and simmer gently for 12–15 minutes. Remove from the heat, but let the chicken cool in the stock.

Peel the cucumbers, reserving some of the skin. Halve them, scoop out the seeds, and place the halves on beds of the lettuce arranged on 4 plates.

Using scissors, cut the drained chicken into thin slivers and arrange these in the cucumber. If preparing in advance, cover and chill.

Make the sauce: Combine all the ingredients except the scallions and sesame seeds in a blender or food processor. Season, then add the scallions and sesame seeds and toss together. Spoon this over the chicken.

Serve garnished with the reserved cucumber peel cut into thin slivers.

PROSCIUTTO AND FRESH FIG SALAD WITH MINT AND LIME CREAM DRESSING

SERVES 6

6 slices of prosciutto
10 fresh mint leaves
juice of 2 limes
18 fresh figs
⅔ cup crème fraîche or sour cream
2 heads of radicchio
salt and freshly ground black pepper
sprigs of mint, for garnish

Cut the prosciutto into strips and cover with plastic wrap to keep it from drying out.

Using a pestle and mortar, bruise and crush the mint leaves in the lime juice. Let the mixture infuse at room temperature about 45 minutes.

Make 2 cuts halfway down each fig from the stem end to make cross-shaped incisions in the top. Press the figs gently in their middles to open up the tops. Place on a plate, cover, and chill 45 minutes.

Remove the mint from the lime juice and discard. Add a pinch of salt to the juice. Gradually whisk in the crème fraîche, stirring constantly. Adjust the seasoning, if necessary.

Flood 6 plates with the crème fraîche dressing. Arrange 3 figs decoratively on each plate. Arrange the prosciutto strips and the salad leaves around them, garnish with the mint sprigs, and serve immediately.

DESSERTS

*M*any cooks tend to overlook the diversity of potential sweet uses of herbs. A whole range of readily available leaves, including mint, lemon balm, and sweet cicely, and flowers, including lavender, geranium, marigold, and elder, make the most delightful accompaniments to a wide variety of summer fruits. Sweet dishes based on dairy products – such as custards, fools and cheesecakes – are good candidates for flavoring with herbs, especially elderflowers, rose petals, lemon balm, and bay. Some herbs like rosemary, geranium leaves, poppy seeds, and aniseed work particularly well in baked dishes such as cakes and cookies, as do the candied leaves and stems such as angelica.

Left: Pear Griestorte with Almonds and Ginger (page 56); center: Spiced Oranges with Lavender and Pine Nuts (page 57)

PEAR GRIESTORTE WITH ALMONDS AND GINGER

SERVES 12–16

butter, for greasing
flour, for dusting
1 cup+2 tbsp granulated sugar, plus more for dusting
6 eggs, separated
grated zest and juice of 1 washed lemon
⅔ cup fine semolina
⅓ cup ground almonds
1 tbsp ground ginger
3 drops of pure vanilla extract
6 ripe pears, peeled and sliced
2 cups whipping cream, whipped to soft peaks
sprigs of mint, for garnish
confectioners' sugar, for dusting (optional)

Preheat the oven to 350°F.

Grease two 8-inch round layer cake pans with butter and line their bottoms with disks of wax paper (this is unnecessary if using nonstick pans). Butter the paper and then dust the paper and the sides of the pans with flour followed by granulated sugar.

In a large bowl, beat the egg yolks and granulated sugar together until pale, creamy, and light. Add the lemon juice and continue beating until the mixture thickens. Stir in the semolina, almonds, ginger, and lemon zest and mix thoroughly. Beat the egg whites to stiff peaks and gently fold them into the batter.

Spoon into the prepared pans and bake 30–40 minutes. The cakes will rise dramatically owing to the proportion of egg to starch. Do not open the oven door or the cakes will subside!

Let the cakes cool, then split them across horizontally. Stir the vanilla extract and some of the pear slices into the whipped cream. Put all the cake layers together with this mixture and then top with the remaining pear slices. Dust with confectioners' sugar, if desired, and decorate with mint.

If preferred, the traditional Austrian layer cake, Griestorte, *can be made as two smaller cakes rather than one big one as described here.* Semolina *is ground from hard durum wheat. It is available, in fine, medium, and coarse grinds, from Italian grocers, health-food stores, and some supermarkets.*

SPICED ORANGES WITH LAVENDER AND PINE NUTS

SERVES 4

4 large, thin-skinned oranges, washed
2 tbsp sugar
¼ tsp ground cinnamon
¼ tsp ground cloves
1 tbsp finely snipped lavender leaves
2 tbsp red currant jelly
2 tbsp pine nuts, toasted

Peel the oranges with a vegetable peeler, reserving the zest of one. Cut the oranges into thin slices and arrange these in a dish.

Put 1¼ cups of water in a pan over medium heat. Add the sugar, cinnamon, and cloves and bring to a boil, stirring constantly to dissolve the sugar. Keep at a low but steady boil until it thickens to a syrup.

Add the lavender leaves, then pour any juices that have drained from the oranges into the syrup. Add the red currant jelly and bring to a boil again.

Cut the orange zest into julienne strips, add these, and boil 3 minutes longer.

Pour the syrup over the oranges, sprinkle with the toasted pine nuts, and serve immediately.

BERRY ZABAGLIONE WITH EAU-DE-COLOGNE MINT★

SERVES 4

3 tbsp fresh berries, puréed
½ tsp minced fresh eau-de-cologne mint leaves
1 tbsp Marsala wine
2½ tbsp sugar
6 egg yolks, beaten
(★see page 2 for advice on eggs)

Strain the berry purée and spoon it into 4 glasses.

Put the mint leaves in a small bowl and pour over the Marsala. Cover and let macerate 1 hour at room temperature.

Place the sugar, egg yolks, and Marsala mixture in the top of a double boiler over hot (not boiling) water. Keep at a moderate heat, beating constantly with a whisk, until thick and creamy. Pour over the purée and serve immediately.

ZABAGLIONE is a frothy Italian custard made from egg yolks beaten with sugar and alcohol. Usually served hot in tall glasses, it is most commonly flavored with Marsala, but some versions use sparkling white wine or even liqueurs.

COULIS *is the French term for a thick sauce or purée, usually of fruit or vegetables.*

STAR ANISE *is a pungent star-shaped spice with a strong aniseed flavor. It is very popular in Chinese cooking and is a constituent in the much-used five-spice powder. It must be used with caution as it can drown the other flavors in a dish.*

PEACHES WITH CHESTNUT AND ROSEMARY PURÉE

SERVES 4

2 tsp fresh rosemary leaves
2 tbsp sweetened chestnut purée
1 cup fresh raspberries
4 large, very ripe sweet peaches, halved, pitted, and peeled
⅔ cup whipping cream, whipped to soft peaks
2 tbsp crushed pistachio nuts

Put the rosemary leaves in a spice grinder or food processor and chop finely. Put this in a strainer and dust it into the chestnut purée. Blend it well into the purée.

Purée the raspberries in the food processor or blender and then push them through a fine strainer to make a raspberry coulis.

Flood 4 chilled plates with the coulis and arrange 2 peach halves on each plate. Cover the peach halves with the chestnut purée, followed by the cream. Finish with the pistachio nuts and serve immediately.

SUMMER FRUITS WITH STAR ANISE AND BORAGE

SERVES 6

1 whole star anise
½ cup sugar
thinly pared zest of 2 washed oranges
⅔ cup light red wine
1 cup red currants
1 cup black currants
1 cup raspberries
1 cup blackberries
1 pint strawberries, halved
10 borage flowers
crème fraîche or sour cream, for serving

Place the star anise, sugar, and orange zest in a pan with ⅔ cup of water and place over low heat. Stir constantly until the sugar dissolves. Then simmer 5 minutes.

Add the wine and bring to a boil. Boil 3 minutes, then cover and simmer 5 minutes. Remove from the heat and let cool. Remove the star anise from the syrup.

Place the fruit in the syrup and toss well to combine. Cover and chill 24 hours.

Just before serving, chop some of the borage flowers and toss these thoroughly into the salad. Garnish with the remaining whole flowers and serve with crème fraîche.

Top: Summer Fruits with Star Anise and Borage; bottom: Peaches with Chestnut and Rosemary Purée

GOLDEN TART WITH ORANGE THYME

SERVES 6

10 tbsp unsalted butter, cut into small pieces,
plus more for greasing
1⅓ cups flour
½ tsp salt
4 egg yolks
½ cup fresh bread crumbs, preferably a mixture of
white and whole wheat
¼ cup golden syrup or light corn syrup
2 tbsp sliced almonds
2 tbsp grated zest and the juice from ½ washed lemon
1 tbsp minced fresh orange-scented thyme leaves

Preheat the oven to 400°F and grease a 9½-inch loose-bottomed tart or quiche pan with butter.

Sift the flour with the salt into a bowl. Add the butter and rub it in with the fingertips until the mixture resembles bread crumbs. Using a fork, mix the egg yolks in lightly, together with enough cold water to make a firm dough.

On a cold lightly floured surface, knead the dough 2 minutes and then roll it out to a thickness of about ⅛ inch. Use it to line the prepared pan and prick the bottom gently with a fork.

Mix the remaining ingredients together and spread them evenly in the pastry shell. Use the pastry trimmings to decorate the top of the tart.

Bake on the middle shelf of the oven until golden, 25–30 minutes. Serve hot, warm, or cold.

Left: Apple Brown Betty with Scented Geranium; right: Golden Tart with Orange Thyme

APPLE BROWN BETTY WITH SCENTED GERANIUM

SERVES 4–6

9 slices of stale whole wheat bread, crusts removed
4 tbsp softened butter
2 lb tart apples, peeled, cored, and sliced
3 tbsp light molasses
1 tbsp minced scented geranium leaves
plain yogurt, custard sauce, or cream, for serving

Preheat the oven to 325°F.

Spread the slices of bread generously with butter and cut each slice into quarters.

Place a layer of one-third of the bread quarters over the bottom of a baking dish. Cover this with half the apple, dribble 1 tablespoon of molasses over, and then sprinkle over half of the geranium leaves.

Repeat with a second similar layer, and finish with a layer of overlapping bread quarters to cover. Spread this with the remaining molasses.

Bake 50 minutes, then increase the temperature to 375°F, and continue baking until crisp and golden brown, about 10 minutes longer. Serve hot, warm, or cold with yogurt, custard sauce, or cream.

MARIGOLD AND APRICOT SORBET★

SERVES 4–6

1 1/4 cups canned apricot halves in syrup, drained
1 egg white, beaten until stiff
(★see page 2 for advice on eggs)
juice of 1 lemon
petals from 2 marigold (calendula) heads

In a saucepan, dissolve the sugar in 2/3 cup water. Bring to a boil and boil until it is syrupy, stirring constantly. Let cool.

Purée the apricots in a blender or food processor, then strain this purée. Stir in the egg white and lemon juice. Then mix this into the syrup.

Put the mixture into an ice-cream machine or in ice-cube trays with half the marigold petals sprinkled into it. If using an ice-cream machine, follow the manufacturer's instructions; otherwise place the trays in the freezer until the sorbet is just set, whisking several times with a fork to disperse large crystals as it freezes.

Serve in chilled glass dishes, decorated with the remaining marigold petals.

PEPPERMINT CREAMS WITH FRESH MINT★

MAKES 24–36

2 cups confectioners' sugar
1 egg white, beaten
(★see page 2 for advice on eggs)
1/2 tbsp minced fresh mint
6 drops of peppermint extract

Sift the sugar into a bowl. Gradually add the egg white, stirring constantly until a stiff paste is formed.

Add the fresh mint and the peppermint extract and combine well. Lightly knead the mixture with the fingertips for 3 minutes.

On a cold surface, roll out the paste to a thickness of 1/4 inch between two pieces of wax paper.

Remove the top sheet of paper. Using a 1-inch round cookie cutter, stamp out the creams, re-rolling trimmings as necessary.

Let dry for 24 hours before serving.

Always invest in the best-quality flavoring EXTRACTS. *Inferior brands are usually synthetic and their flavor can mar a dish.*

GOOSEBERRY FOOL WITH ELDERFLOWERS

SERVES 4

1 ½ pints gooseberries
½ – ¾ cup sugar
5 elderflower heads
⅔ cup whipping cream, lightly whipped
almond cookies, for serving (optional)

FOR THE CUSTARD SAUCE

1 egg
⅔ cup milk
2 tbsp sugar
1 tsp pure vanilla extract

Place the gooseberries in a pan with the sugar, 3 elderflower heads, and 2 tablespoons of water. Cover and simmer until the fruit is completely soft. Remove from the heat and let cool.

Remove and discard 2 of the elderflower heads, then process the mixture to a smooth purée and strain it.

Make the custard: Combine the egg, milk, and sugar in a heavy saucepan. Cook over low heat, stirring constantly, until the custard thickens enough to coat the back of the spoon. Remove from the heat, stir in the vanilla, and let cool, stirring occasionally.

Fold the cream into the gooseberry purée, followed by the custard, combining them well. Chill at least 2 hours. Serve garnished with the remaining elderflowers and accompanied by almond cookies.

Left to right: Peppermint Creams with Fresh Mint (page 61), Marigold and Apricot Sorbet (page 61), and Gooseberry Fool with Elderflowers

ELDERFLOWERS
*(the flowers of the
elder tree) have the
useful property of
neutralizing the
acidity of other
ingredients. It is for
this reason that they
are cooked with
sharp fruit, such as
rhubarb and citrus
fruits. Elderflowers
also have the
advantage of being
free to those lucky
enough to have a
tree growing in
their yard.*

INDEX

Page numbers in *italic* refer to the photographs